"The discovery of a new dish does more for human happiness
than the discovery of a star."

Jean Anthelme Brillat-Savarin

DEDICATION AND ACKNOWLEDGEMENTS

To my wife, Yvonne and our four children, Mary Louise, Chris, Mark and James, whose liking for brandied dishes helped make this book possible.

To the California Brandy Advisory Board and Jim McManus, its president, for valuable guidance, help and counsel.

To my friends who volunteered their brandy recipes.

To Gordon Bennett of Gordon Bennett & Associates, whose assistance brought the book to reality.

The First BRANDY Cookbook

by Malcolm R. Hebert

Illustrated by Mike Nelson

Table of Contents

Joys of Cooking With Brandy

You hold in your hand the first cookbook devoted exclusively to cooking with brandy. While it is a source of satisfaction to have created the first brandy cookbook, it is a pity that such a book has not previously been available, for the joys of cooking with brandy are many.

Americans of taste almost everywhere are enjoying a sustained love affair with cooking old dishes and new, with more sophistication and style than did their forefathers.

In our quest for different and more exciting recipes, many of us have turned to cooking with wines and spirits and, in my opinion, there is no better spirit with which to cook than brandy. The excitement of brandy in cooking is the sometimes subtle, sometimes pronounced, but always unique flavor it lends to otherwise less interesting dishes. Happily, the flavor of brandy blends with and improves almost all foods.

Brandy is a joyful ingredient in gourmet cooking because of the flavor it contributes, and because it gives you opportunities for dramatic flaming service at

2

your table.

There are no secrets to successful flaming with brandy, but there are simple techniques. Most 80 proof brandy will ignite readily if it is at room temperature. You can guarantee repeated success if you warm the brandy slightly by pouring it carefully into the warm juices or sauce of the dish to be flamed and igniting it. You can use a match, or light it by tipping the pan or chafing dish forward carefully to allow the flame from the burner to set afire the brandy fumes. For an added touch of color, try sprinkling a little granulated sugar in the flames for a beautiful blue-violet effect.

If there is more liquid in the pan than just enough to cover the ingredients it may be difficult, if not impossible, to ignite the brandy. In such cases I forego the flaming and happily settle for the flavor.

When preparing desserts with several different liqueurs—including brandy—always add the brandy last and light it immediately.

This book contains no recipes for vegetables with brandy. This is not by accident, but by design. In my experience, vegetables are not elevated in taste by the addition of brandy. I remember once being served a spinach salad with bacon bits, red wine vinegar and flamed with brandy. No brandy flavor at all. My host was obviously reaching for showmanship alone—which for me is not enough.

I hope that you will read the recipes with interest and that you will be moved to try them. I hope that you will feel free to vary the combinations and amounts of flavor to your own special tastes, so that you will be creating new recipes and thereby enjoying the greatest pleasure any cook can experience through your own creativity.

The recipes are easy to follow; you need no special ingredients and there are no long, complicated procedures. Most of them are either my own or my adaptations of other recipes which I have used in my own kitchen; several of them have been in my family for generations.

My sincere hope is that you, too, will find it fun and rewarding to cook with brandy, and that this book will stimulate you to experiment, to invent, and to create your own exciting brandy dishes.

Good Luck and Good Eating!

Malcolm R. Hebert

The First Course

The words "hors d'oeuvres" translate literally to "out of work," and in derived usage, to something like "so good and out of the ordinary that only small portions should be served." Americans with plainer tastes in language call the same dishes "appetizers." However called, these small servings are intended to prepare the palate for more important things to come.

Brandy adds interest, flavor, and excitement to the beginning foods you offer your guests. In the pages immediately following, you will find a sampling of ways to use brandy with olives, cheeses, shrimp, mushrooms, and some meats; but there are many more. Try these and then go on to your own inventions.

One caution: unless you want your guests to blunt their appetites, do not serve more than three appetizers before the meal and I believe that, at any one serving, only one of these three should be brandied.

BRANDIED OLIVES

This simple appetizer is easy to prepare well in advance of the party.

One 15 oz. (drained weight) jar of green olives
brandy

Drain the liquid from the jar but do not remove the olives. Refill the jar to the top with brandy, reseal and refrigerate for at least 8 hours. Then taste one olive. It should taste just right, but if you like a still more pronounced brandy flavor, simply leave the olives in the jar longer. This size jar will contain about 50 large olives. Obviously, you may use any size jar you need—the proportions of olives to brandy will be the same.

BRANDY ROQUEFORT SPREAD

Light cheese spreads go nicely for a cocktail party or as a pre-dinner appetizer.

This is one of my favorites.

1 lb. Roquefort cheese
1/2 cup butter
1/3 cup brandy
a pinch of cayenne pepper
1/4 cup finely minced onion

Mix cheese and butter together until smooth and creamy, using your blender or a fork. Add brandy, pepper and onion and blend into a smooth paste. Spread on Melba toast or crackers, or serve in a small bowl and let your guests prepare their own. This will keep for several weeks if stored in small jars in your refrigerator. Makes a little over 3 cups.

MUSHROOMS MONTEBELLO

Almost everyone likes mushrooms and here is a new way to serve them. This marinade not only adds refreshing flavor but appears to "cook" the mushrooms without heat.

1/2 lb. fresh mushrooms, small button variety
1/2 teaspoon crushed oregano
salt & pepper to taste
1/4 cup olive oil
1 clove of garlic, crushed
1 tablespoon brandy
2 tablespoons red wine vinegar
a pinch of dill weed

Cut the stems from the mushrooms and reserve for another use. (They can be chopped fine, mixed with homemade mayonnaise and spread on thin Melba toast.) Wash the mushroom caps thoroughly, dry, and cut in half. Mix all of the

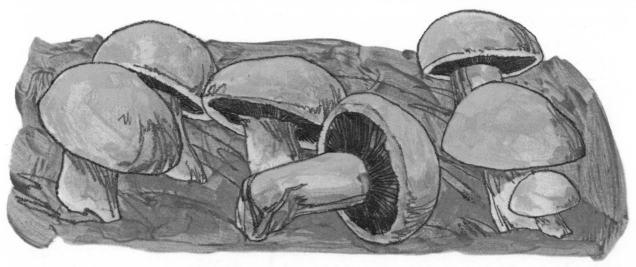

remaining ingredients together in a bowl, add the mushroom caps and toss until all are thoroughly coated with the marinade. Let stand at room temperature for about an hour. Serve with toothpicks. Enough for about 8 people.

TARTARE STEAK GENGHIS KHAN

The brandy and garlic in this recipe combine to create a new and original Tartare appetizer.

1 lb. of freshly ground sirloin
1/2 cup of finely chopped onions
1 clove of garlic, mashed
salt & pepper to taste
1 whole egg
1 tablespoon of brandy

Mix everything together well—with your hands is easiest. You can serve it: formed into individual meatballs, about 1/2 inch in diameter, with cocktail picks; or mounded handsomely on a plate with toast rounds. Serves 10.

MOZZARELLA IN CAROZZA

12 slices of stale, firm, white bread
6 slices Mozzarella cheese, same size as the bread
3 eggs
1/2 cup milk
1 tablespoon brandy
2 cups of fine bread crumbs

Trim the crusts from the bread slices and make sandwiches with bread and cheese. Beat the eggs lightly and add milk and brandy; dip the sandwiches into this batter and then into bread crumbs. Fry in 1 inch of hot olive oil. When crisp on the outside, drain on a paper towel, cut into quarters or triangles and serve hot. Serves 6.

Soups

Everyone enjoys soup—from a clear consomme to a thick nourishing gumbo—they are universally a part of the human diet. Every culture has given us at least one (and usually many) variety of soup indigenous to its people. Recipes for soup have been handed down to us from the kitchens of kings and the hovels of peasants.

A good soup sets the tone of a meal and the addition of brandy makes for exciting beginnings.

The French have put brandy to good use in soups for generations, as have adventuresome cooks in western America. Brandy gives soup a special flavor regardless of the amount used.

Brandies taste different because of the difference in blending—one distiller will blend for a dry brandy while another will blend for a mellow taste. Once you find the particular brandy which suits your taste, stay with it—in soups and in all your cooking.

CONSOMME DE FOIE GRAS

This elegant brandied soup can be found in some of the world's great restaurants.

5 cups chicken broth
Two 1/2 inch slices of foie gras, cubed
1/3 cup brandy
2/3 cup Port

Bring the chicken stock to a boil and add the foie gras. Remove from the heat and add brandy and Port. Let stand for a few minutes to infuse the flavors. Serves 6.

POOR MAN'S MINESTRONE

Brandy adds taste and interest to humble soups as well, as proven by this simple minestrone.

4 large onions, chopped fine
3 tablespoons butter
1/2 cup of broken vermicelli or spaghetti
3 tablespoons tomato paste
1-1/2 quarts chicken stock
1/4 cup brandy

In a saucepan, saute onions in butter until soft, add vermicelli or spaghetti and cook until light brown in color, stirring often. Add remaining ingredients, bring to a boil, reduce heat, and simmer for about 10 minutes. Serve with grated cheese. Serves 6.

BRANDY CONSOMME

Another simple, clear soup: consomme, a few herbs and a little brandy warm the body and the spirit on a winter's day.

6 cups beef broth
1/4 cup brandy
1 pinch each of basil, dill, thyme, and tarragon
grated cheese or sour cream

Put everything into a two quart saucepan and bring to a boil. Lower heat and simmer for 10 minutes. Let rest for one minute and serve with grated cheese or a spoonful of sour cream. Serves 6.

COLD APPLE SOUP

Here's a cold soup for a hot day. If you like the taste of apples, you'll love this chilled refresher.

1-1/2 lbs. of apples, peeled, seeded, and cut into small cubes
water to cover
sugar to taste
juice of 1 lemon
1/4 cup brandy

Simmer the apples in water to cover, along with the sugar and lemon juice. When the apples are cooked, about 20 minutes, press them through a sieve. Then mix in the brandy, which will thin the soup a little. Refrigerate until cold and serve. Serves 4.

CIOPPINO SAN FRANCISCO STYLE

San Franciscans love this justly famous fish soup. Serve it with a green salad and French bread. Give everyone a bib to wear and put the pot right on the table for second helpings. This is such a filling and nourishing dish, you can serve it as a main course. (See menu on page 170.)

1 large onion, chopped fine
1/4 cup olive oil
one 1 lb.-14 oz. can of tomatoes, chopped fine, plus the liquid
one 6 oz. can tomato paste
1-1/4 cups dry white wine
3 cups water
1/4 cup brandy
1/2 teaspoon each of thyme, oregano, and coarsely ground black pepper
1 bay leaf, crumbled
3 crabs, cracked

1 lb. scallops, cut in half
1 lb. small shrimp, shelled and deveined
24 clams in the shell

Saute the onions in the olive oil, using a very large pot, until lightly browned. Add tomatoes, tomato paste, wine, water, brandy and seasonings. Cover and simmer for 2 hours. Add seafood and cook for another 10 minutes or until shellfish are done. To serve, divide the fish portions equally into large soup bowls and pour the sauce over them. Serves 12.

START WITH A NAIL

Once upon a time a stranger came to town and, in the middle of the square, set up a large kettle over a roaring fire. He filled the kettle with water and from his robe took a large nail and dropped it into the kettle. When asked what he was making, he replied, "I am making nail soup."

The townspeople gathered about him to watch. He tasted the water with the nail in it and said, "How much better this soup would taste if I had an old bone to put into the kettle." Someone in the crowd produced an old bone and the stranger dropped it into the kettle. He tasted the soup again and expressed the thought that a carrot would add much flavor. An onlooker gave him a carrot.

He tasted again and mused aloud that perhaps a piece of meat, some celery, a clove of garlic, and a little drop of brandy would enhance the flavor. All were offered for the pot.

Pronouncing the soup ready, he let the townspeople taste it. They all nodded their heads saying, "Yes, you can make fine soup from a nail." . . . and you can too, with or without the nail.

NAIL SOUP

1 10 oz. can of beef stock
1 can of water (use the beef stock can)
1/2 cup each, chopped carrots & celery
1 cup chopped onions
1 pinch each, basil, thyme, oregano
1/2 cup dry red wine
1/4 cup brandy
1/2 lb. lean beef, cut into 1/2 inch cubes

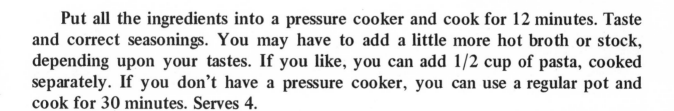

Put all the ingredients into a pressure cooker and cook for 12 minutes. Taste and correct seasonings. You may have to add a little more hot broth or stock, depending upon your tastes. If you like, you can add 1/2 cup of pasta, cooked separately. If you don't have a pressure cooker, you can use a regular pot and cook for 30 minutes. Serves 4.

ONION SOUP

Brandy and onion soup are soul mates—each flavor enhances the other, and this recipe is a particularly happy combination of the two.

2 cups thinly sliced onions, (preferably Italian red)
1/2 cup butter
1-1/2 quarts of rich beef stock
1/4 cup brandy
1/2 cup freshly grated Parmesan cheese

Saute the onions in the butter until soft and golden. Add beef stock and brandy and cook over high heat for 10 minutes. Add cheese and serve. Serves 6.

24

LENTIL SOUP HEBERT

This thick, hearty soup is easily made in the pressure cooker.

1 cup dry lentils
2 cups chicken stock
2 cups water
1/4 cup of diced, blanched salt pork
1/2 cup of carrots, diced
1 cup of diced onions
1 clove of garlic, crushed
1 bay leaf
salt and pepper, to taste
1 peeled, chopped tomato
1/4 cup brandy

Put everything into a pressure cooker and cook for 12-15 minutes. Top with freshly grated Romano cheese. Serves 6.

Meats

Brandy gives meat dishes a gourmet touch. Brandy can be used in a marinade; a few tablespoons of brandy can be added to the meat during preparation; or brandy can be used to flame the dish as an exciting serving technique. Experiment a little with the amounts of brandy suggested in these recipes, and vary the quantity used to suit your personal taste.

Almost all 80 proof brandies will flame easily when warmed. To be sure that it will flame, heat the brandy in a small pan, light it and then pour it over the food.

PEPPER STEAK

A good steak flavored with pepper, brandy, and butter is one of life's great pleasures . . . and is easy to prepare for any number of guests.

6 small steaks, preferably filets or tenderloins
4 tablespoons of coarsely cracked pepper
6 tablespoons butter
2 ounces brandy

Press cracked pepper into both sides of the steaks, cover them with waxed paper and refrigerate for 2 hours. Remove from refrigerator and allow meat to come to room temperature (about 1 hour). In a large skillet melt 4 tablespoons of butter and saute the steaks until done to your taste. Pour off the excess butter and remove the steaks to a warm platter. Put the remaining two tablespoons of butter and the brandy into the skillet, turn the heat high and stir up all the brown particles. Cook for 30 seconds and then strain the sauce over the steaks. Serves 6.

STEAK DIANE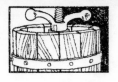

Here is a classic dish, using a choice cut of beef, which you prepare in your chafing dish right in front of your guests.

1 sirloin steak, 1-1/2 to 2 lbs. about 1 inch thick
4 tablespoons butter
1 medium onion, chopped fine
1/4 cup brandy

In the kitchen, cut the uncooked steak diagonally into 8 strips about a half inch in width. At the table, cook the onions in butter in the chafing dish until soft. Add the strips of steak and saute until done to your taste, then remove them to a warm platter. Pour the brandy into the pan and ignite; swirl the pan around to loosen all the brown particles and when the flame dies out, pour the sauce over the meat and serve immediately. Serves 4.

STEAKS IN PURGATORY

This easy-to-prepare dish offers you almost infinite opportunities for variation.*

1/4 cup flour
6 small steaks,
    sirloin if possible, 1 inch thick
6 tomatoes, peeled, seeded and chopped

1/4 cup olive oil
1/4 cup chopped parsley
1/2 teaspoon freshly ground pepper
2 tablespoons brandy

Flour steaks. In a large skillet over high heat, brown the steaks quickly, then remove steaks and cook the tomatoes, olive oil, parsley, pepper, and brandy until the tomatoes are almost reduced to a puree. Add the steaks and cook to your taste: rare—5 to 8 minutes; medium—8 to 10 minutes; well done—anything after 12 minutes. Serve on buttered toast with a little of the sauce.

*Variations: add a clove of garlic for an Italian touch; curry for an Indian touch; Sherry along with the brandy for a Spanish effect; the combinations are endless. Serves 6.

30

BRANDY MARINATED STEAK

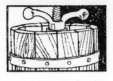

If you prefer marinated meats you'll find this savory brandy marinade to your liking.

6 medium size steaks
1/2 cup brandy
1/2 cup dry red wine
Juice of 1 lemon
2 cloves of garlic, crushed
2 onions, finely chopped
2 carrots, finely chopped
Pinch each of tarragon, basil, and oregano
1 bay leaf

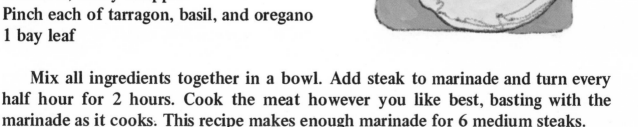

Mix all ingredients together in a bowl. Add steak to marinade and turn every half hour for 2 hours. Cook the meat however you like best, basting with the marinade as it cooks. This recipe makes enough marinade for 6 medium steaks.

 # STEWS AND RAGOUTS THE WORLD OVER

In every country of the world there is a ragout or stew to satisfy the best and biggest appetites.

Germans never eat a ragout without noodles; the French insist on their stew being cooked in red wine and/or brandy; the Russians garnish their stews with sour cream; the Hungarians are in love with their paprika; the Italians like pasta in their stews; and the Irish add potatoes, while the Indians eat their stews with rice.

Stews and ragouts give the cook a golden opportunity to improvise -- vary the ingredients to please family preferences in vegetables and meats, experiment with seasonings, try new combinations using vegetables you may not have served before. Create, serve, and enjoy!

BASIC BEEF STEW

Ragouts and stews originate from a basic dish containing beef, butter, wine, brandy, vegetables and seasonings. From this basic recipe you can experiment to suit your personal tastes.

3 lbs. of stew meat, trimmed of all fat
4 tablespoons butter
1-1/2 tablespoons flour
salt & pepper
1/4 cup brandy

2 cups chopped onions
Pinch of parsley and thyme
3 cups beef bouillon
3 cups water

Cut beef into cubes and brown in the butter using a heavy skillet or Dutch oven. Sprinkle flour on the meat and stir it until the flour is slightly brown. Add the remaining ingredients and bring to a quick boil. Then lower the heat, cover and simmer for 1-1/2 hours. Skim off excess fat and remove the meat; keep it in a warm place. Taste sauce, adjust seasonings and pour over the meat. Serves 6.

BEEF STEW VARIATIONS

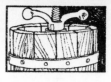

With slight changes in the basic recipe, you can make these gourmet versions.

BEEF BURGUNDY

Eliminate the 3 cups of water and add 3 cups of Burgundy along with 1-1/2 cups of cooked mushrooms and 1/2 cup of diced cooked bacon.

BEEF PROVENCALE

Add two cloves of minced garlic, 1/2 cup of dry white wine, 2 small diced carrots and 1/2 cup diced tomatoes.

BEEF STRASBOURG

Make a puree with 1/4 cup of cream and 1-1/2 tablespoons of pate de foie gras. Add to the stew 5 minutes before serving, stirring in gently.

CHOCOLATE BEEF STEW

For a truly unique stew, try this specially flavored Spanish entree.

3 lbs. of pot roast, cut into cubes
3 tablespoons olive oil
1 large onion, chopped fine
3 cloves of garlic, chopped fine
1 teaspoon salt
1 tablespoon flour
2 bay leaves

1 cup dry white wine
1/2 cup beef broth
1/2 cup water
1/4 cup brandy
1 tablespoon white wine vinegar
1 tablespoon grated bitter chocolate

Braise meat in the olive oil, using a deep kettle. Add onion and garlic and cook until the onions are soft, then stir in salt and flour, mixing well. Add all remaining ingredients except the chocolate. Cover tightly and simmer over low heat 2 to 2-1/2 hours. Remove meat to a warm platter. Skim the fat from the sauce, add grated chocolate and whisk until mixed. Strain, and serve sauce separately. Serves 6.

BRANDY POT ROAST

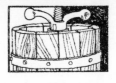

This recipe is so simple, people sometimes wonder if it really works. Actually, it is neither roast nor stew, but a unique way of cooking this nutritious—but occasionally tough— cut of meat.

During cooking, check the pan often, making certain that there are enough juices in the pan so the meat does not stick to the pan. You may add spices and herbs to suit your individual taste.

4 lbs. pot roast	1 peeled clove of garlic	1 teaspoon tarragon
1/2 cup olive oil	1 teaspoon salt	1 teaspoon basil
1/3 cup brandy	1 teaspoon pepper	3/4 cup red wine

Place the roast in a Dutch oven. Combine oil and brandy and pour over roast. Sear meat on all sides and let cook, covered, over low heat for about 1 hour. Check every 1/2 hour for liquid content. If low, add more brandy. After the first hour, add garlic, salt, pepper, tarragon, basil and red wine. Simmer for another hour. When meat is tender, remove, strain juices, and serve. Serves 6.

STUFATINO DI MANZO

Here is an Italian version of beef stew with a happy combination of red wine and brandy.

2-1/2 lbs. of lean beef, cut into cubes
3 tablespoons olive oil
1/4 lb. of blanched, diced bacon
1 large onion, sliced
2 cloves of minced garlic

a pinch each of marjoram and rosemary
2/3 cup red wine
2 tablespoons brandy
4 tablespoons tomato paste
salt and pepper to taste

Heat oil in a large skillet and saute the bacon, onion, and garlic for 3 to 4 minutes. Add the beef, marjoram, and rosemary and cook until the beef cubes are browned. Dilute the tomato paste with the wine and brandy, add to the stew along with enough water to cover the meat and cook for 2 hours over medium heat. Just before serving, add an additional dash of red wine. Serves 6.

SHORT RIBS SATANIC

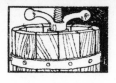

A quick dish which invites a crisp, cool salad, a bottle of red wine, French bread and a hearty appetite.

3 lbs. short ribs of beef,
  cut into 3 inch serving pieces
2 tablespoons Dijon mustard
salt to taste
1/2 teaspoon chile powder
1/2 teaspoon sugar

juice of a small lemon
1/4 cup olive oil
1 small garlic clove, crushed
1 small onion, chopped fine
1/3 cup brandy
1/3 cup beef bouillon

Place the short ribs in a deep bowl, add all the ingredients, cover, and marinate in the refrigerator for several hours. Drain and reserve the marinade. Preheat your oven to 425° and bake ribs for 30 minutes on a rack in a roasting pan. Reduce heat to 325° and baste with marinade every 10 minutes for 1-1/2 hours. Skim off all the fat from the pan and serve the beef with the remaining marinade. Serves 6.

POTTED ROAST

Potted roast or beef is an English term, more often associated with the famed Potted Shrimp so well loved in England. There are just about as many recipes for English potted shrimp as there are Englishmen. Most culinary historians suggest that the word "potted" came from the fact that shrimps were pounded to a fine paste and then put into small pots and served as an individual first course. In light of this the name "Potted Roast" may not be historically correct, but you will be pleased with the results.

1 five lb. boned roast of beef
flour
1/4 cup butter
1/2 cup each, chopped carrots, onions and leeks
1 crushed clove of garlic
2 cups dry red wine
1 bay leaf

40

1/4 teaspoon each of thyme and marjoram
2 tablespoons brandy
salt & pepper to taste

Preheat your oven to 325°. Dredge the roast in flour. In a Dutch oven, heat the butter and brown the roast; add carrots, onions, and leeks and saute until brown. Add everything else but the brandy. Ignite the warmed brandy and pour over the roast. When flame dies out, cover and bake in the oven for about 2-1/2 hours. Transfer the meat to a warm platter; strain and correct seasonings in the sauce. Serve sauce separately. Serves 6.

GARLIC LAMB

Garlic is a conventional seasoning for lamb—but add brandy and wine! You produce an unconventional delight.

1 leg of lamb, about 5 lbs.
butter, salt and pepper
8 unpeeled cloves of garlic
1 bottle of dry white wine
1/4 cup brandy

Trim all fat from the leg of lamb. Rub the roast all over with butter, salt, and pepper. Into a medium size roasting pan, put garlic, wine and brandy. Place the leg of lamb on a rack and set it in the pan. Pierce the meat a number of times with a fork. Roast in a 325° oven, basting the lamb with the drippings every 20 minutes. When your meat thermometer registers "lamb done" or 180°, the meat is ready. Serve sauce separately.

LAMB CHOPS NICHOLAS

Chops, too, can be made glamorous through the addition of brandy and wine.

8 small rib lamb chops
3 tablespoons olive oil
1 small clove of garlic, crushed
2 tablespoons chicken broth
3 tablespoons dry white wine
1 tablespoon brandy
1 tablespoon tomato paste
1/2 teaspoon crushed tarragon leaves

In a skillet, saute the chops in olive oil until done, then remove to a warm serving platter. Add to the pan the garlic, wine, chicken broth, brandy, tomato paste, and tarragon. Bring to a boil, turn down the heat, and simmer for 5 minutes. Remove from the heat, strain, and pour over the chops. Serves 4.

VEAL LODI

Here's another simple and delicious way to prepare veal with just butter and brandy, and a pinch of dill.

8 very thin slices of veal
3 tablespoons butter
2 tablespoons brandy
pinch of dill

Melt the butter and mix with brandy and dill. Brush liberally over the veal and saute in a small amount of butter over medium heat. Add salt and pepper to taste. Serves 4.

As a variation you can use thin slices of turkey breast (raw) instead of the veal.

LEMON VEAL SCALLOPINE

This is an exceptional dish for a light, simple menu. You can serve a light soup; the veal, which cooks quickly in butter, oil and brandy; a salad with almost any kind of dressing; and a dessert mousse to complete the meal. Perfection!

1-1/2 lbs. veal pounded thin to make a scallopine
6 tablespoons butter
flour
2 tablespoons each of olive oil and lemon juice
1/4 teaspoon grated lemon rind
2 tablespoons lemon juice
brandy
tarragon

Dust the scallopine in flour and quickly saute them in the butter and olive oil. Add grated lemon rind, lemon juice, and simmer for 3 to 4 minutes. Remove to a heated serving platter and add a dash of brandy. Thin lemon slices may be used for garnish. Serves 4.

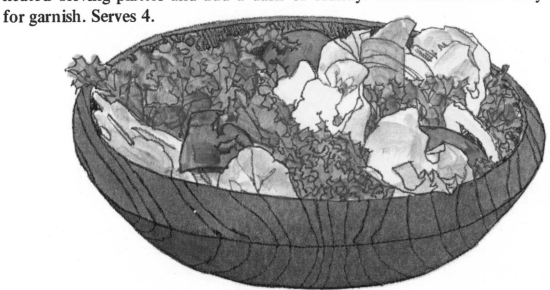

COUNTRY PATÉ

One of the finest of all picnic dishes is a paté. Not the kind you buy in a can, but a homemade paté with spices, brandy, salt, and pepper. Homemade patés are easy to make, eat and serve.

1/2 lb. veal
1/2 lb. pork
1/4 lb. ham
11 slices of uncooked bacon
2 cloves of garlic, minced
1/2 cup brandy
1 egg
1/2 teaspoon each of basil, salt, and pepper

Grind the first three items and 4 slices of blanched (boil in water for 5 minutes) bacon very fine. Line a small casserole or paté mold with the remaining raw bacon, leaving 1/2"of each slice over the side of the dish. In a bowl, add the seasonings, garlic, brandy, and egg to the ground meat and mix well. Fill the mold, packing it tightly, fold the bacon ends over the top and bake for one hour in a 325° oven. Refrigerate overnight. You can unmold it just before you leave or you can carry it to your picnic in the baking dish. It is best served in 1/2 inch slices with French bread. Serves 4.

SPECIAL NOTE: Gourmets have often tried to match a perfect pate with a perfect wine. Some prefer a red wine such as California Cabernet Sauvignon, while still others insist on a sweet white wine. My suggestion is--try both and then decide for yourself.

BRANDY GLAZED HAM

A simple ham glaze becomes elegant via the addition of brandy to basic ingredients.

1 smoked or ready-to-eat ham
1 cup brown sugar
3 tablespoons prepared mustard
1/2 cup brandy.

Put the ham, fat side up, in a shallow roasting pan. Bake in a 325° oven. If you use a smoked ham, allow 25 minutes per pound; ready-to-eat ham needs only 15 minutes per pound. Forty-five minutes before the ham is done, take it out of the oven, remove the rind and score the fat in both directions. Mix brown sugar, mustard, and brandy into a paste and spread liberally over the top and sides of the ham. Return the ham to the oven to continue cooking. Brush ham with the glaze mixture about every 10 minutes until done. Serves 8.

LOIN OF PORK WITH BRANDIED PRUNES

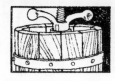

A pork roast stuffed with brandy-soaked prunes is a superlative dish and is attractive and appetite-appealing when placed on the table ready for serving.

one 4-5 lb. loin of pork
20 pitted prunes
1/2 cup of brandy
salt and pepper to taste

Have your butcher (or do it yourself) bone the loin and cut a pocket in the center lengthwise. Soak the prunes in the brandy until soft—about 3 hours. Drain, reserve the brandy, and insert the prunes in the pocket of the loin. Season the meat with salt and pepper, then tie the loin into a round shape using string. In a small Dutch oven, brown the meat on all sides, basting every ten minutes with the brandy marinade. Cook for 3-1/2 hours over low heat, covered, adding liquid as required. (I use chicken stock.) Serve the loin sliced, with the pan juices and drippings in a sauceboat. Serves 6.

BRANDY SAUSAGE

If you have never made, cooked, and eaten your own homemade sausage, then you have been missing one of the great taste treats of your life. Nothing, absolutely nothing, can ever take the place of homemade sausage—and, once you have tasted your own homemade sausage, no commercial brand will ever taste as good.

6 lbs. of lean fresh pork
1/2 teaspoon red pepper
1-1/2 tablespoons salt
1/2 tablespoon freshly ground pepper
3/4 tablespoon sage
1/2 cup brandy
5 yards of sausage casing

Cut the pork into cubes and grind, using the fine blade in your meat grinder.

Add all the seasonings, making certain they are evenly mixed into the meat; then sprinkle the brandy over the mixture and work it in—the easiest way is to use your hands for the mixing.

Attach sausage stuffer to the grinder and, using about a yard of casing at a time, start stuffing the casing by re-feeding the meat through the grinder into the casing. Twist or tie into links. Keep refrigerated because the sausages are perishable. You can freeze them for longer storage. This will provide about 50 3-inch sausages.

Seafoods

Brandy is a versatile aid to seafood cookery. In this section, it is flamed in three recipes; adds a delicious flavor to the sauce in five; and contributes bouquet and aroma to the steaming liquid in the case of mussels and clams.

With these recipes, as with those in the other sections of this book, I urge you to experiment with a variety of brandies. The lighter, drier brandies will give a different taste to a dish from that of the mellower, heavier brandies. You may find that with some combinations of spices, herbs, and condiments you will prefer one type of brandy, while with a wholly different combination of other seasonings, another brandy will please you more. With several different brandies on your kitchen shelf, you can become a chef and connoisseur.

BRANDY LOBSTER

For extremely simple preparation, it is difficult to surpass this brandy lobster.

three 2 to 3 lb. lobsters
salt and pepper
12 tablespoons of softened butter
1/2 cup brandy

Split the lobsters in half, remove the eyes and the sac behind them; remove the intestines and break the claws. Most fish merchants will be glad to do this for you if you don't choose to do it yourself. Place the lobsters, shell side down, in a baking pan and season with salt and pepper. Put 2 tablespoons of the softened butter on each half and bake in a 450° oven for 12 to 15 minutes. Remove the baked lobsters to a heated serving platter and carry to the table. Pour warmed brandy over them and ignite. Serve immediately after the flame dies. Serves 6.

FILET FLAMBE

While sole is presently the most popular fish being served on American tables, there are many other fish that fit the bill-of-fare quite adequately. In fact, it is surprising that many recipes are so strict about the fish to be used when indeed other fish lend themselves to the same method of preparation. In this recipe, filets of sole are called for, but there is no reason why ling cod, red snapper, or lemon sole cannot be substituted.

6 medium size fresh filets of sole
salt and pepper, to taste
paprika
1-1/2 tablespoons brandy
1-1/2 tablespoons Pernod

Rub the filets with salt, pepper, and paprika. Place in well-buttered pan and broil until done (flakes easily with a fork). Warm mixture of brandy and Pernod, pour over fish, and flame. When flame dies, serve. Serves 6.

COLD BOUILLABAISSE

This version of the fish soup, for which Marsellaise is quite justly famous, served cold on a warm summer's day makes a delightful one-dish meal and should be a new experience for you.

1/2 lb. lobster meat, uncooked
12 raw shrimp, peeled and deveined
1 lb. each of bass, halibut, and lemon sole, cut into 2 inch pieces
12 mussels in the shell
12 clams in the shell
3 cloves of garlic, minced
1/2 cup olive oil
1 cup dry white wine
4 tablespoons shallots or baby green onions, chopped
3 tablespoons brandy
1/2 cup tomato paste
2 cups water

You can make this dish in an hour—including the time needed to cool it. In a large pot, combine all the ingredients and cook over medium heat for 10 to 12 minutes. Cool the bouillabaisse in your refrigerator for 30 to 40 minutes and serve. Some cooks like to take a little longer and simmer the cooking base (wine, brandy, olive oil, etc.) for 15 minutes before they add the fish and the shellfish. Mussels or clams which do not open during cooking should be discarded. Serves 6.

 # FILET OF SOLE – BRANDY & BITTERS

The delicate flavor and tender taste of sole should not be masked by stronger flavors. The grapes, brandy and bitters in this recipe provide perfect complements to the fish.

1/2 cup flour
6 tablespoons butter
4 medium filets of sole
1 cup of seedless grapes
2 tablespoons brandy
3 to 4 dashes of Angostura bitters

Dust the fish with flour and saute in 3 tablespoons of the butter. When the fish is cooked, remove to a heated serving platter. Put the remaining butter in the pan, add the grapes and cook for 2 minutes over medium heat. Add the brandy and the bitters, heat through, and pour over the sole. Serves 4.

VINTNER SHRIMP

All too frequently shrimp are over-sauced, over-battered and over-cooked. Here's one recipe that treats the shrimp properly.

2 lbs. raw, peeled and deveined shrimp
1/2 cup olive oil
1 tablespoon brandy
1 clove of garlic, minced
1/8 cup of minced parsley

In a medium size skillet, saute the shrimp in half the oil and all of the brandy. When cooked (about 3 to 4 minutes) remove to a heated serving platter. To the pan, add the balance of the oil, the garlic and parsley, then simmer for just a scant minute more. Pour over the shrimp and serve. Serves 6.

SHRIMPS YVONNE

The basil and the garlic in this recipe give the shrimp a flavor you may never have experienced before. It is good with dried basil, but better if you use the fresh leaves.

3-4 lbs. of tiny shrimp, peeled & deveined
6 tomatoes, peeled, seeded & chopped
1/2 cups fresh basil,
   or 2 tablespoons of dried

salt and pepper
4 cloves of garlic, chopped
2 tablespoons brandy
1 cup olive oil

Cook the shrimp in boiling water, just enough to cover, for 2 to 3 minutes. Drain, spread them out on a large serving platter and place in a warm oven. Put the garlic, basil, salt, and pepper into your blender and run at moderate speed until mixed; add the tomatoes and brandy and blend. Finally, add the oil and continue blending until the entire mixture is smooth. This sauce can be poured over the shrimp, coating them well before serving, or you can let your guests help themselves from a sauceboat. Serves 8.

CRAB MENDOCINO

Here is a crab main dish with the delightful effects of flamed brandy and dry white wine for a very satisfying Sunday lunch.

4 slices bacon
2 onions, finely chopped
1 clove of garlic, minced
2 tomatoes, peeled, seeded and chopped
1 teaspoon dried basil

1 lb. cooked crabmeat
1/4 cup brandy
3 tablespoons tomato puree
2 cups dry white wine
parsley, salt & pepper to taste

In a large skillet saute the bacon until crisp. Crumble and set aside. In the remaining bacon fat, saute onions and garlic until soft, then add tomatoes, basil, salt, and pepper; cook over low heat until blended. Add the crabmeat. Pour warm brandy over the mixture and light it. When the flame dies, add the tomato puree, wine, and parsley. Cook briefly until well blended, about 2 minutes. Garnish each individual serving with crumbled bacon. Serves 4.

CRAB GUICHET

Cold crab, like cold shrimp, is often served with a hot peppery tomato sauce that overwhelms the delicate taste of the seafood. The first lesson a chef learns is to increase or heighten the natural taste of the food being prepared. Here is an old Creole method of doing just that—without the peppered tomato sauce!

1 lb. cooked crab meat, chilled
1 teaspoon brandy
1 tablespoon homemade mayonnaise (if possible)
1 cup dry bread crumbs

Flake crab meat rather fine. Combine with all other ingredients, mix well, and form into 4 heart-shaped patties. You may find it necessary to alter the amounts of brandy and bread crumbs slightly, depending on the moisture content of the crab. Broil the patties for 3-4 minutes and serve with Monterey Sauce, page 103.

 # MARINATED MUSSELS

On a warm summer day or when you seek a light repast, here is a simple recipe for serving mussels as a first course.

24 mussels, medium size, well scrubbed and washed
1/2 cup dry white wine
2 tablespoons brandy
1 bay leaf
1/2 stalk of celery, chopped fine
2 tablespoons olive oil
1 tablespoon fresh lemon juice
1 teaspoon fresh dill
1/8 teaspoon sugar
salt & pepper to taste

Trim the beards off the mussels and steam them in a deep kettle with the wine, brandy, bay leaf, and celery. They should be done in 5 to 7 minutes.

Remove them from the pot and chill. Discard any mussels that did not open during cooking. To the remaining liquid, add olive oil, lemon juice, the dill, sugar, salt and pepper to taste. Pour over the chilled mussels and let them marinate overnight. Serve in the shells. Serves 4.

MUSSELS LAGUNA

The mussels in this recipe are served hot and make a very satisfactory main dish which, accompanied simply by a crisp salad, is a total experience.

60 mussels, medium size, well scrubbed and washed
1 cup dry white wine
1/2 cup water
2 tablespoons brandy
1 tablespoon of chopped white onions
1 sprig of parsley
1/4 of a bay leaf
1 clove of garlic, minced
3 tablespoons butter
1 tablespoon of chopped parsley
salt and pepper to taste

Put the mussels in a deep kettle or pan and add the wine, water, brandy, onions, parsley, bay leaf and garlic. Cover tightly and cook over high heat for 5 to 6 minutes, or until all the shells have opened. Remove mussels from the liquid; discard any that have not opened (they are not good) and then discard one shell from each of those remaining, leaving the other with the meat in it. Set them aside on a warm platter or in a warm oven. Now add the butter to the liquid and cook over medium heat until it is reduced to 1/2 the original quantity. Taste for seasoning and add salt, pepper, and chopped parsley. In deep soup bowls serve 10 mussels per person and pour the sauce directly over the shellfish. Serve generous quantities of fresh French bread for soaking up the sauce. Serves 6.

STEAMED CLAMS

Steamed clams have been with us for generations—served with clam broth and melted butter. The addition of brandy in this recipe heightens both the flavor and the fragrance.

60 washed and scrubbed clams
salted water
2 tablespoons brandy
melted butter

Put the scrubbed clams in a large kettle with salted water an inch deep, and add the brandy. Cover and steam until the clams are open, discarding those that remain closed. Serve the clams still in their shells in individual bowls, 10 to each bowl. Strain the broth through several layers of cheesecloth and serve it, and also the melted butter, in individual bowls. Serves 6.

CRAYFISH IN CREAM

The crayfish (pronounced crawfish) is often called a baby lobster because it is considerably smaller and more tender than its briny brother. For this particular recipe you should allow at least 12 crayfish per person.

72 crayfish
2 qts. lightly salted water
4 tablespoons butter
salt & pepper
3 tablespoons brandy
3 tablespoons finely chopped onions
2 tablespoons finely chopped parsley
a pinch of thyme
1/2 bay leaf
1/4 cup tomato puree
1-1/2 cups dry white wine
2/3 cup of cream

In a large pot boil the crayfish in two quarts of lightly salted water for 8 to 10 minutes. Drain and peel them, reserving the meat from the tails. Set aside and keep warm. In a saucepan, heat the butter and flame with 2 tablespoons of heated brandy. When the flame dies, add the onions, salt, pepper, parsley, thyme, bay leaf, tomato puree, and the wine. Cook mixture over medium heat for 10 minutes and reduce to about 3/4 of the original volume. Add cream, the remaining tablespoon of brandy and pour over the crayfish tails. Serves 6.

Fowl

The more usual varieties of fowl such as chicken, turkey, and duck are high in protein and reasonably priced. The delicate flavor of poultry lends itself to the addition of a variety of seasonings and accompaniments. In planning a menu with fowl as the entree, the selection of salads and companion dishes is relatively easy as many vegetables and fruits combine well with its mild taste.

The ways to cook fowl are many and varied—they can be roasted on a spit, steamed, cooked in cream, sauteed, pan roasted, basted as they cook, or complemented with a sauce when served. With each of these ways, the use of brandy creates new and delicious flavors. On the pages immediately following you will find innovative ways to prepare chicken, game hens, duck, and pheasant—all with the added attraction of brandy.

 # BASTING SAUCES

Sauces heighten the flavor of any fowl cooked over charcoal.

BRANDY & BUTTER

Combine equal portions of melted butter and brandy. Brush bird or birds liberally every 8 to 10 minutes.

BUTTER, BRANDY & ANISE

Mix as above, but add 2 teaspoons aniseed. For a more intense flavor of anise put 1 teaspoon of aniseeds with a little of the butter and brandy mixture inside the bird—and baste, too.

OLIVE OIL, BRANDY & OREGANO

Baste with equal parts olive oil and brandy plus 1 tablespoon of oregano.

BUTTER, BRANDY & THYME

Same as the previous sauce except substitute 1 tablespoon of thyme for the oregano.

RED WINE, BRANDY & BUTTER

Mix 1/2 cup each of red wine, brandy, and melted butter. Mix thoroughly and brush on the bird frequently.

BRANDY, KETCHUP & OLIVE OIL

Mix together 1/2 cup each of brandy, ketchup, and olive oil and brush on the bird.

If you want to save yourself the effort of frequent bastings, the bird will baste itself—from the inside out, but the flavor will be milder. Cut the proportions of any one of these six recipes in half and place the mixture inside the bird's cavity.

CHICKEN O'FARREL

Cooking "en papillote" (in a paper bag) seals in the juices and steams the chicken. The brandy, the apple and the clove in this recipe combine to create a special and unique flavor.

1 whole chicken, about 3 lbs.
1 apple, cored
1 clove
2 tablespoons brandy
salt & pepper
salad oil
1 paper bag

Cut the apple into quarters, stick the clove into one of the quarters and place them, along with the brandy, salt, and pepper, into the chicken's cavity. Truss the bird as for roasting. Moisten the paper bag all over the outside with salad oil. Put the trussed chicken into the oiled bag, fold the top shut and secure with paper

78

clips. Bake in a shallow pan at 325° for about one hour. Remove from the oven, open the bag (be careful of the hot paper clips!), remove the chicken, carve and serve. The juices in the bag can be poured over the chicken servings. Serves 4.

CHICKEN BREASTS WITH BRANDY

This rich, smooth dish requires only the firm press of a fork for eating. Serve with fresh French-cut green beans, barely cooked—white wine and candlelight.

3 whole chicken breasts, boned and halved
salt & pepper
1/4 cup brandy
1/4 cup butter
1 cup heavy cream
minced parsley

Salt and pepper the chicken breasts, then saute in melted butter until lightly browned. Heat the brandy and pour it over the chicken and light it. When the flame dies, add cream, cover, and simmer for 15 minutes. Remove the chicken to a heated serving platter; taste the sauce, correct the seasoning, and strain over the chicken breasts. Garnish with minced parsley. Serves 6.

CHICKEN IN PARADISE

The boning and skinning required in preparing the chicken breasts for cooking is well worth the added effort. Brandy in combination with the four complementary seasonings makes this a hearty main dish.

6 chicken breasts, skinned, boned, and pounded thin—as for scallopine
1/4 cup olive oil
4 tablespoons butter
6 cloves of garlic cut in half
2 medium size bay leaves
1/2 teaspoon dried thyme
salt & pepper to taste
2 tablespoons red wine vinegar
2 tablespoons brandy
1/2 cup chicken stock

In a large skillet, heat the oil and butter and add the garlic, bay leaves, thyme, salt, and pepper. When the mixture is sizzling, add the chicken breasts and cook for 4 to 7 minutes—depending on the size and thickness of the meat. When done, remove to a warm platter and place in a warm oven. Now add the vinegar and the brandy to the skillet, cook for 2 minutes, then add the chicken stock. Scrape loose all the brown bits in the bottom of the pan, mixing the sauce well. Strain through a fine mesh tea strainer and pour over the chicken breasts. Serves 6.

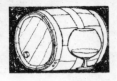

TARRAGON CHICKEN

Tarragon is an herb which perfumes with authority, yet with a gentleness seldom found in other herbs. If you have fresh tarragon leaves, tuck a few into the cavity of a fowl you are cooking whole. This will give a fine and unusual flavor to the meat. This recipe achieves a similar result, although the chicken is halved and sauteed.

2 fryers, halved, about 2 lbs. each
1/3 cup flour
1 teaspoon each of salt and pepper
4 tablespoons butter
4 tablespoons fresh tarragon (or 2 tablespoons of dry tarragon)
1/4 cup dry white wine
2 tablespoons brandy

Put the flour, seasoned with salt and pepper, into a paper bag with the chickens and thoroughly coat them. Melt the butter in a skillet and saute the chicken for 30 to 45 minutes. Remove from the pan and sprinkle tarragon on both sides of all four pieces. Now place the chickens in a casserole, pour the blended wine and brandy over them, and bake in a 450° oven for 5 to 8 minutes. Remove chickens to a warmed platter and strain the sauce over them. Serves 4.

MUSCAT HENS

Since brandy is made from wine and wine is made from grapes, it seems appropriate to include in this book recipes utilizing grapes. This one calls for muscats and the recipe on page 92, for Thompson seedless.

4 Cornish hens
1 medium size bunch of muscat grapes, pierced
one split clove of garlic
salt and pepper
2 tablespoons brandy

Wash the hens and dry them carefully. Rub their cavities with salt and pepper and rub the skins with the split clove of garlic. Divide the pierced grapes into 4 bunches and stuff one bunch into each bird. Truss and roast in a 450° oven for 20 minutes. Reduce the heat to 350°, pour off the fat in the bottom of the roasting pan, return to the oven and baste with brandy every ten minutes for 30 minutes. Remove hens from the pan, discard the grape stuffing, and cut the birds into serving portions. Skim the fat from the sauce in the roasting pan again, and pour sauce over the individual servings. Serves 4.

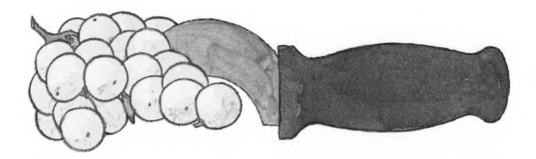

CHICKEN SAUTE SIMON

Because of the time required for cooking, you will start with the chafing dish in the kitchen, then bring it to the table for serving.

one 3 lb. fryer, cut up
salt and pepper
1/3 cup butter
1/3 cup chopped onions

1/4 cup chopped parsley
1/2 teaspoon marjoram
1/4 cup of fresh lemon juice
1/4 cup brandy

In the chafing dish, heat the butter until it froths and then add the salted and peppered chicken pieces. Put in onions, parsley, marjoram, and saute for about 5 minutes. Add heated brandy and ignite it. When the flame dies, add the lemon juice and cook for another 20 minutes or until the chicken is tender. Serve directly from the chafing dish, spooning the sauce over each serving. Serves 4.

CORNISH HENS ROYALE

Cornish hens are America's answer to those hundreds of little game birds the Europeans enjoy. Commercially grown Cornish hens have more flavor than their larger cousin, the chicken. The most common cooking method for Cornish hens is spit-roasting, but here is a fresh approach that enhances the rare taste of bird.

3 Cornish hens, halved
3 large cloves of garlic, peeled, halved
3 tablespoons olive oil
1 tablespoon butter
1 teaspoon brandy

Into a large saute pan, put the garlic, oil, butter, and brandy and heat. When very hot, add hens and saute until done, turning frequently to brown all over. When done, remove pieces to a warm platter. Remove garlic, strain oil and serve separately. Serves 6.

CHICKEN CHRISTOPHER

You could call this "quick chicken with brandy" because from start to finish, the whole process takes a scant 30 minutes.

1 medium size fryer, cut up
salt & pepper to taste
3 tablespoons butter
1/4 cup brandy
1 pinch dill weed

Salt and pepper the chicken pieces. Melt the butter in a heavy skillet, add dill weed and saute the chicken until it is evenly browned. Heat the brandy and pour over the chicken; ignite and spoon the flaming liquid over the chicken until the flame dies out. Cover and cook for 20 minutes or until tender. Serves 4.

THOMPSON CHICKEN

Seedless grapes and tarragon in stuffing for the bird make this entree different—and delectable. Basting with brandy alters the flavor of the meat and contributes much to the taste of the sauce.

one 4 to 5 lb. roasting chicken
6 slices dry, crumbled bread
2 chopped onions
1 cup of Thompson seedless grapes, chopped
6 tablespoons melted butter

1/2 teaspoon finely minced parsley
1/4 teaspoon tarragon
salt and pepper, to taste
chicken stock to moisten stuffing
1/4 cup brandy

Make a stuffing by combining the bread, onions, grapes, butter, parsley, tarragon, salt, and pepper. Add enough chicken stock to moisten the stuffing. Taste, correct the seasonings, and stuff the chicken. Truss and roast in a 350° oven for 1-1/2 to 2 hours, basting frequently with the brandy. Remove to a serving platter, carve, and spoon out the stuffing. Pour the basting sauce and juices over both chicken and stuffing. Serves 4.

DUCK WITH BRANDY MARINADE

When you marinate duck this way, you thoroughly infuse the bird with enhancing flavors. This marinade also works very well with other fowl.

2 domestic ducks, 3 to 4 lbs., cut up
1 pinch of nutmeg
salt & pepper
2 medium onions, finely chopped
1 clove of garlic, finely chopped
1/2 cup brandy
1/2 cup red wine
1 pinch marjoram

Put the cut-up duck and the rest of the ingredients into a deep bowl. Allow to marinate for at least two hours, turning the pieces every 20 minutes. Grill the duck over very hot charcoal, basting each piece with the remaining marinade. Serves 6.

ROAST DUCK WITH PEACH GARNISH

Here is a straightforward way to roast a duck, but the simple garnish makes the completed entree extraordinary.

one 4 to 5 lb. duckling
salt and pepper

First, score the skin of the bird with a sharp knife at 1 inch intervals. Rub the cavity with salt and pepper (you may include other seasonings, if you wish). Roast uncovered and unbasted, using a shallow roasting pan in a 325° oven. It should take 2-1/2 to 3 hours and is done when the legs can be moved up and down easily. When you serve, don't try to carve, but use poultry shears or a knife to cut serving portions. Place portions on a warmed platter.

FOR THE GARNISH:

4 canned peach halves
1/4 cup brandy
3 tablespoons sugar
1 tablespoon butter
1/3 cup cider vinegar
1 cup of liquid from the can of peaches
1/2 teaspoon arrowroot dissolved in 1 tablespoon of water

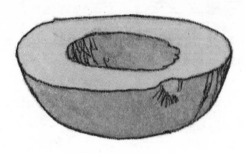

Marinate the peach halves in brandy for 1/2 hour, turning them several times. Melt the butter and sugar in a saucepan and cook until mixture is brown. Add vinegar and continue cooking until mixture is reduced to one-half the original volume. Add the peach liquid; thicken with the arrowroot and simmer another 10 minutes. Five minutes before serving, add the peaches and brandy to the sauce. Spoon over individual portions of duck. Makes enough for 4 servings.

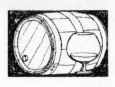

PHEASANT QUENELLES

Because pheasant meat tends to be dry when roasted, I have created this moist, tender entree which should make for well-satisfied dinner guests.

one 3 lb. pheasant
1/2 lb. of pork shoulder
1 teaspoon salt
pepper
1/4 cup brandy

1/4 cup white wine
1/4 lb. butter, melted
1/4 cup heavy cream
3 egg yolks

Remove meat from the pheasant and discard the skin and bones. Put the meat, the pork shoulder, salt and pepper through the medium blade of your meat grinder. Use a large bowl to marinate this mixture in brandy and wine for one hour. Then add the melted butter, cream, and egg yolks, mixing together until smooth. Your blender will do it best.

Now bring the 2 cups of chicken stock to a boil (you will use this for the sauce—see facing page). Dip two tablespoons in ice water. Use one to scoop up a spoonful of the meat mixture and with the other spoon mold the mixture, making small egg-shaped quenelles. Drop these into the boiling chicken stock and cook for 10 to 12 minutes. Remove and place on a heated serving platter.

SAUCE:

2 cups chicken stock
1/4 cup Madeira
4 tablespoons butter
4 tablespoons flour

Using the pan in which you cooked the quenelles, reduce the stock to 1-3/4 cups, then add the wine. In a separate pan, melt the butter, add the flour and mix well. Slowly add the chicken/red wine stock to the butter/flour mixture and cook for several minutes until thickened. Pour over the quenelles and serve. Serves 6.

Sauces & Salad Dressings

If you do not generally include sauces in your menus, it is time for you to try—for the difference is truly in the sauce, and vive la difference! Once you have made the simpler sauces as given here, you will be encouraged to go on to preparation of the more complex ones.

Almost everyone knows that the great chefs of the world often establish their reputations on their sauces and, in many instances, these sauces literally take days of preparation. Great chefs can, and do, take days to create their superb sauces—it is their art and their livelihood. Neither you nor I need try to compete, but without taking days to do it, we can provide sauces which make some dishes spectacular.

What follows on the next thirteen pages are uncomplicated adornments using brandy in small amounts—just enough to give your entrees a professional touch.

WINE MERCHANT'S SAUCE

2 teaspoons finely chopped shallots, or green onions
2/3 cup red wine
1 tablespoon brandy
1/4 cup butter
1 teaspoon chopped parsley
salt & pepper

Simmer shallots (or onions) and wine in a small skillet until mixture is reduced to 1/4 its original volume. Let it cool. In another pan melt butter and add to wine/shallot mixture. Add the remaining ingredients and stir. Taste and correct the seasoning. Serve with broiled meat. Enough for 6 steaks.

SAUSALITO SAUCE

2 tablespoons of green onions, chopped
2 tablespoons butter
1/2 tablespoon chopped parsley
1 bay leaf
1/2 cup red wine
1 tablespoon brandy
1 cup beef stock or broth

Simmer the onions in butter using a small pan. When they are soft, add the remaining ingredients and continue cooking until the sauce is half its original volume. This is excellent with broiled meats. If you need a sauce for veal, fish or chicken, use white wine instead of red.

BRANDY BARBECUE SAUCE

1 cup dry red wine
1/2 cup brandy
1 cup olive oil
1/2 tablespoons salt
1 large red onion, grated
1 large clove of garlic, crushed
pinch each of pepper, tarragon, and thyme

Mix all ingredients together in a small bowl. Cover and refrigerate for 24 hours, then use for basting chops, steaks, roast—whatever you like to barbecue.

MONTEREY SAUCE

4 cups stewed tomatoes, or 1 No. 2-1/2 can
1 teaspoon olive oil
2 tablespoons butter
2 onions, minced
1 clove of garlic, minced
1 tablespoon each, chopped chervil and parsley
2 tablespoons brandy

In a medium saucepan, cook tomatoes until almost all the liquid has cooked away and then puree them in your blender or press through a sieve and set aside. In a small skillet, heat the olive oil and butter and saute onions, garlic, chervil, and parsley. Add the tomato puree. Cook over medium heat for about 5 minutes, then add brandy and cook for another 2 minutes. Use this happily with any seafood dish. Serves 6.

BRANDY SALAD DRESSING

3 tablespoons olive oil
1 tablespoon red wine vinegar
salt & pepper
1 tablespoon brandy
1/2 tablespoon crushed tarragon
1/2 tablespoon dill weed

    Mix all ingredients together in a jar or bowl, pour over your favorite salad greens, and toss thoroughly.

BRANDY MAYONNAISE (Master Recipe)

2 egg yolks, raw
1/2 teaspoon salt
1/2 teaspoon dry mustard
1 tablespoon tarragon wine vinegar
1 tablespoon brandy
1 cup olive oil

In your blender, mix the first five ingredients at high speed for no more than 1/2 minute. Turn to slow speed and add the olive oil, slowly, through the small opening in the lid of the blender until the entire mixture is smooth and thick. This recipe makes approximately 1-1/2 cups of mayonnaise.

The following are four cheese variations for Basic Brandy Mayonnaise.

ROQUEFORT DRESSING

To the master recipe simply add 1/4 cup of crumbled Roquefort cheese just before the mayonnaise is done.

STILTON DRESSING

To the master receipe add 1/4 cup of crumbled English Stilton cheese.

ROMANO DRESSING

To the master recipe add 2 tablespoons of grated Romano cheese.

Butters can be used in many ways—added to soups and sauces, spread on steaks and chops, mixed with salads and greens—the choice is yours.

BRANDY BUTTER

Cream 1/2 lb. of salted butter with 2 tablespoons of brandy. Spread on steaks, other broiled meats, or drop into soups just before serving.

ALMOND BUTTER

Pound 1/2 cup of blanched almonds to a paste and put into a small bowl. Add 2 teaspoons brandy (more if you like) and gradually mix in 1/4 lb. of soft salted butter. When blended, rub the mixture through a fine sieve. Add to cream sauces or spread on broiled chicken.

GARLIC BUTTER

Peel 6 whole cloves of garlic and boil for 6 minutes. Drain and crush them. In a small bowl or blender, mix the crushed garlic with 6 tablespoons of creamed butter and 1 tablespoon of brandy. Mix thoroughly. Use as a spread with oysters and seafood entrees.

SHALLOT BUTTER

Parboil 4 teaspoons of finely chopped shallots in 1/2 cup of water for 2 to 3 minutes. Drain, dry, and crush the shallots; mix with 6 tablespoons of creamed butter and 1 tablespoon of brandy. Use on steaks or broiled fish.

TRUFFLES

Truffles are a delicacy found underground, usually under oak trees, mostly in Europe (the best ones come only from a couple of areas in France and Italy), and are used in preparing fowl, in pastries, and can be served various ways by themselves.

Truffles are readily (if expensively) obtainable in most specialty food stores in America. Recently the canned truffle trimmings have become available at about 40 percent of the cost for canned whole truffles. These trimmings have all of the delicate flavor and aroma of the whole ones and lend themselves well to recipes like the one on the facing page.

Buy a small can of these trimmings, open it immediately, pour the contents into a small glass jar and fill it with brandy. This will preserve the truffle trimmings and enhance their flavor. You can preserve them this way and use small amounts over a long period of time.

TRUFFLE SAUCE

1 tablespooon truffle trimmings, preserved in brandy
4 tablespoons butter
salt & pepper to taste
1 teaspoon brandy
1 cup Veloute sauce (see next page)

Gently saute the truffle trimmings in 2 tablespoons of butter for 2 minutes. Season with salt and pepper, pour the warmed brandy over the truffles and ignite. When the flame dies, add the Veloute sauce. Mix well, then stir in the remaining 2 tablespoons of butter to smooth the sauce. Serve with game birds or chicken. Makes enough sauce to serve 6.

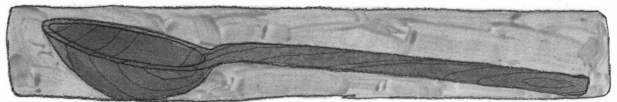

VELOUTE SAUCE

This is how you make the sauce needed as an ingredient in the Truffle Sauce on page 111.

4 tablespoons butter
4 tablespoons flour
2 cups chicken stock

Heat the butter in a small pan and when it has completely melted, add the flour and mix well. Cook for only a couple of minutes, then add the chicken stock. Cook over medium heat until thick and creamy.

CALIFORNIA STYLE VINAIGRETTE SAUCE

This is a variation of the classic Vinaigrette sauce, using brandy.

1 tablespoon brandy
3 tablespoons olive oil
1/4 teaspoon dry mustard
salt & pepper to taste
a few drops of red wine vinegar
1 teaspoon mixed dry herbs, including tarragon, parsley, chives and chervil

Mix all ingredients well in a jar or bowl, chill and pour over fish, meat, or vegetables—served either hot or cold, or over salads.

Desserts

The basic rule of coordinating dessert with the rest of the meal is: a rich dessert with a light meal—a light dessert following a heavy, rich meal. In this era of weight-consciousness, most people seem to prefer the light dessert on the majority of occasions. The considerate hostess or host will plan meals with the dietary preferences of guests in mind.

Here are light and airy—rich and substantial—cold and refreshing—hot and warming desserts—and they all include brandy with delectable results. From this collection, you will find one to enhance any menu you plan. Those dishes which call for flaming the brandy can complete your meals with grace, dignity and showmanship. Of the twenty recipes in this section, brandy adds both flame and flavor to five and flavor alone to fifteen.

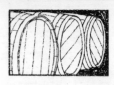

FLAMING BANANAS HEBERT

For a dramatic finale to your meal, prepare this at the table using your chafing dish.

6 ripe bananas, sliced lengthwise
juice of 1/2 a lemon
1/4 cup butter
1 cup brown sugar
3 dashes of cinnamon
1/4 cup brandy
ice cream of your choice

Brush peeled bananas with the lemon juice and set aside. Melt butter in a chafing dish, add brown sugar and cinnamon, When sugar is dissolved, add bananas and cook until tender -- about 3 to 5 minutes, Warm the brandy in a ladle, light it and pour over the bananas. When the flame dies, serve two banana slices on each side of a scoop of ice cream and spoon sauce over each serving. Serves 6.

ORANGE BRANDY ICE

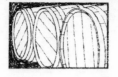

Ices, those refreshers of yesterday which signaled the next course was about to begin, have reappeared on the culinary scene. Today, in keeping with the trend toward careful weight control, we use them in place of rich, creamy desserts. Here is a new recipe for an ice in which brandy plays its part.

2 cups of sugar
4 cups of water
1 cup of orange juice
1 cup of brandy
1/4 cup of lemon juice
finely grated rind of two oranges

Combine sugar and water in a saucepan and boil for 5 minutes. Cool slightly and add remaining ingredients. Cool, strain, and freeze in individual parfait glasses. Serves 6.

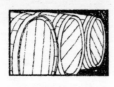

CHOCOLATE CREAM POTS

This is a rich, delicious dessert which gains much from only a touch of brandy.

1 6 oz. package of semi-sweet chocolate bits
1 tablespoon sugar
1 egg
1 teaspoon vanilla extract
1 teaspoon brandy
3/4 cup milk

Place the chocolate, sugar, egg, vanilla, and brandy in a blender but don't turn it on yet. Heat the milk in a small saucepan, bring to a boil and pour immediately over the contents of the blender. Now cover and blend at high speed for one minute. Pour this creamy mixture into six small custard cups and chill in the refrigerator for at least two hours. Top with unsweetened whipped cream, if you like.

118

ITALIAN CHRISTMAS COOKIES

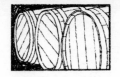

Cookies are welcome at any time of the day by any age group. Occasionally, after a very large meal, cookies and a small glass of wine are preferable to a rich dessert. This old Italian cookie recipe, blending the flavors of brandy and pignolia nuts, will fit such a situation perfectly.

1/2 cup softened butter
1 tablespoon sugar
3 tablespoons honey

1 cup flour
2 tablespoons brandy
1/2 cup chopped pignolia nuts

Combine softened butter, sugar and honey. Cream thoroughly, then add all remaining ingredients and mix until you have a smooth pastry. On a lightly floured board, spread the pastry—using your hands—until about 1/2 inch thick. With a sharp knife, cut one-inch squares and place them 1 inch apart on a greased cookie sheet. Bake at 375° for about 10 minutes. Makes about 30 cookies.

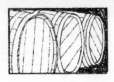

ZABAGLIONE

A traditional Italian dessert, this is served in most fine Italian restaurants—but not usually with brandy. It does make a difference.

4 egg yolks
4 tablespoons sugar
8 tablespoons Marsala (an Italian dessert wine)
4 tablespoons brandy

Put the egg yolks, sugar and Marsala in the top of a double boiler, heat over water and whisk. Add the brandy and beat until thick and fluffy. Pour into small dessert glasses and top each with lemon rind zest. (One stroke of an unpeeled lemon on the finest side of your grater will give you quite enough zest for each serving.) Serve warm. Serves 4.

BRANDY SOUFFLE

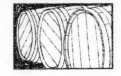

I once wrote an article on souffles for WINE magazine, the official journal of the International Food and Wine Society, in which I said: "I love souffles. To me a souffle is the most perfect of all known desserts. I have had many encounters with souffles and each time I have been seduced by their taste, their richness and their beauty."

With this recipe, my seduction is complete.

3 eggs, separated
4 tablespoons powdered sugar
2 tablespoons brandy

1 pinch of salt
additional sugar
butter

Beat the egg yolks until light, add sugar, brandy, salt, and mix well. In a separate bowl, beat the egg whites until they peak. Now fold the egg whites into the yolk mixture. Butter a souffle dish and sprinkle the bottom and sides with sugar, shaking out any excess. Pour souffle mixture into the prepared dish and sprinkle the top with a little sugar. Bake in a 350° oven for 45 minutes. Serves 4.

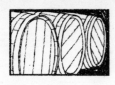

BRANDY BINGS

Since it is derived from fruit itself, it is logical that brandy is a complement to many other fruits. This simple ice cream topping is a fine example.

1 lb. of pitted Bing cherries (fresh, if possible)
1/2 cup currant jelly
1/4 cup brandy

Mix everything together thoroughly. The brandy will dilute and mix with the jelly very quickly. Refrigerate for at least three hours and then pour over ice cream of your choice. Serves 4.

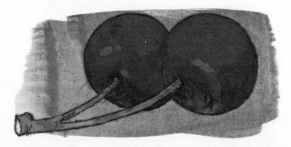

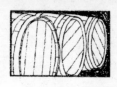

ICE BRANDY GRAPES

These will sparkle and glisten—and you can eat them with your fingers if you wish.

1 large bunch of Thompson seedless grapes
2 egg whites
1 tablespoon brandy
granulated sugar

Separate the grapes into edible clusters—3 or 4 grapes each. In a small bowl, whip the brandy and the egg whites lightly with a wire whisk, but do not foam them. Dip the grape clusters into the egg and brandy mixture and sprin'.le liberally with sugar. Refrigerate for 2 hours and serve as finger desserts. Serv s 6.

FIRE PEACHES

Here again, fruity brandy adds flavor and flaming color to otherwise plain peaches.

1 No. 2-1/2 can of cling peaches
3 tablespoons butter
1 teaspoon sugar
1/4 cup brandy

Put the butter, sugar and half of the juice from the canned peaches into a warm chafing dish. Cook for one minute to make a sauce; then add the peaches and stir gently to coat with the sauce. Warm the brandy, ignite and pour over the peaches. Serve as soon as the flame dies. Serves 4.

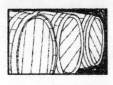

FRUIT FLAMBES

This retains all the fine fruit flavors while blending smoothly with sugar, butter and brandy. The dish is best with fresh fruit but still very good with canned.

enough fruit for six people (peaches, pears, apricots and cherries)
1/2 cup butter
1/2 cup sugar
juice of one large orange, strained
2 tablespoons brandy

When you use fresh fruit, peel and core the pears, peel the peaches and remove the pit, remove pits from the apricots and cherries. Heat the butter in a deep pan, add sugar and orange juice and cook over medium heat until the sugar has melted. Add the fruits and continue to heat gently, turning the fruit a number

of times to coat completely with the sauce. Pour in warmed brandy and ignite it. When the flame dies, serve in shallow dessert dishes or in sherbet glasses. Spoon the sauce over each serving. If your chafing dish is large enough, you can do this at the table. You can also vary the combination of fruit according to taste and availability.

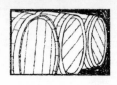

APPLE SPREAD

Many people search for the "perfect dessert." Some consider it to be the souffle; others relish cheese and a glass of red wine.

But there is one dessert that can please all palates. It is simple, easy and delicious. I share it with you here.

1/2 lb. Roquefort cheese, crumbled
8 oz. (1 package) softened cream cheese
1/2 cup finely chopped pecans
1/2 cup brandy
large red apples

Let all the ingredients stand at room temperature for about an hour. Then mix together well with a fork or in a blender at low speed, until smooth. Peel several large red apples, cut them into bite size wedges (remove the core), then spread the cheese mixture over the apples and serve with Cream Sherry.

FROZEN BRANDY MOUSSE

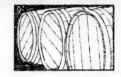

One of the glamour desserts that adds the perfect "fini" to a special dinner is the frozen mousse. This little added attraction can be frozen in the freezer compartment of your refrigerator or in your home freezer. Mousses can be frozen in fluted paper cups, individual small souffle molds or in one large mold. Complete freezing takes from 2 to 4 hours, depending on the type of container you choose.

6 egg yolks
1/2 cup sugar
1 cup heavy cream
1/4 cup brandy

Beat egg yolks and sugar until well blended. Add cream and brandy. Beat the mixture over a large bowl of cracked ice (keeps the mixture cold) until frothy. Pour into individual molds and freeze. Serves 6.

CAFE BRULOT

This is the famous dessert drink from New Orleans.

1-1/2 cups brandy
1 small cinnamon stick
1 small vanilla bean, whole
5 cubes of sugar
1 slice each of lemon peel and orange peel
2 cups of very strong, very hot coffee

In a chafing dish, mix everything but the coffee and heat until warm. Pour an additional ounce of brandy into a ladle and light it. As it burns, lower the ladle into the chafing dish, igniting the warm mixture. Now slowly pour the coffee into the pan and use the ladle as a blender, moving it gently back and forth through the flaming liquid. When the flame dies out, serve in demitasse cups. Serves 8.

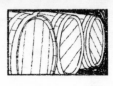

STRAWBERRIES IN CHAMPAGNE & BRANDY

Fill a tulip champagne glass with five or six fresh medium-size strawberries. Pour dry champagne into the glass to within 1/2 inch of the top, then add 2 tablespoons brandy and chill for 30 minutes in the refrigerator. You and your guests can eat the berries with a spoon and feel free to drink from the glass when the berries are gone.

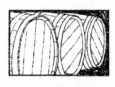

APRICOT BRANDY

1 cup dried apricots   1 cup water
1 cup sugar   1 cup brandy

Combine ingredients and put into a 1-quart jar. Store in a cool place. Taste after six weeks. Use as suggested for Vanilla Brandy, page 133. This brandy is also delightful spooned over vanilla ice cream and apricot halves or slices.

132

VANILLA BRANDY

This simple gastronomic delight is, in itself, a master of disguise. It can be served as an after dinner liqueur; infused into whipped cream; used as a topping for ice cream; ladled over a fruit cake; incorporated into cakes, pies, and puddings.

2 whole vanilla beans
1/2 bottle brandy

Cut the vanilla beans into 2-inch pieces and split the pods open. Put them into the brandy bottle, reseal, and store for 2 to 3 months.

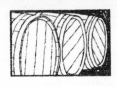

DESSERT OMELETTES

Dessert omelettes are not as familiar to most cooks as are omelettes served as a first course, main course, or as a side dish. Ancient Romans used the name "ova mellita" to define eggs beaten with honey and cooked in an earthenware dish. Some historians think this name evolved over the period of years to "omelette."

When should you serve an omelette as a dessert?

A great deal depends upon the main course. If the menu is light—summerish— a dessert omelette is very much in order. Let your own food and menu preferences guide you.

FRITTATE DOLCE CON LA MARMELLATA

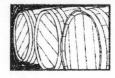

While this Italian dessert omelette features apricot jam, almost any jam you like can be substituted.

6 eggs	3 tablespoons butter
3 teaspoons water	4 tablespoons apricot jam
salt	granulated sugar
grated rind of half a lemon	1/4 cup brandy

With a fork, beat the eggs together with the water for half a minute. Add a pinch of salt and the lemon rind. Melt the butter in an omelette pan and, when foam stops, add the eggs. When the omelette is set, turn it out onto a warm flat plate. If necessary, add a little butter to the pan, turn the omelette back into the pan and cook the other side until done. Do not overcook! Slip the omelette onto a board and spread the apricot jam evenly on top. Roll it up and put it on a heatproof platter, sprinkling sugar over it. Pour warmed brandy over the omelette and ignite it. When the flame dies out, serve. Serves 6.

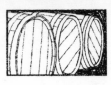

FRUITCAKE & BRANDY

Fruitcake is a great American dessert which dates back to the Pilgrims. It is probably the single dessert that is served most often in homes and restaurants in the U.S. during the holiday season.

Brandy plays an important role in elevating fruitcake to the position it holds in the minds and tastes of gourmets. My Grandmother, and probably yours, poured several ounces of brandy over the fruitcake every two or three days for weeks at a time until the cake literally burst with goodness.

Often fruitcake is eaten without adornment. Some people like to spread it with butter and accompany it with a Cream Sherry or Port.

A sauce for fruitcake is less conventional but it's here—on the facing page—and it is delicious.

SAUCE MARY LOUISE

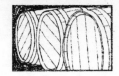

1-1/3 cups powdered sugar
1/2 cup butter
salt
1 egg, separated
3 tablespoons brandy
1/2 cup whipped cream

Let the butter stand in a warm kitchen for about an hour. When softened, blend in the sugar, add a pinch of salt and the egg yolk. Cook in the top of a double boiler over warm water, constantly stirring to keep the mixture from burning. In 6 or 7 minutes the mixture should be light and fluffy. Remove from the heat, stir in the brandy, then chill in the refrigerator for 20 minutes. In the meantime, beat the egg white until it has soft peaks. When the first mixture is chilled, fold in the beaten egg white. Just before serving, fold in the whipped cream and spoon over slices of fruitcake. Serves 6, amply.

HARD SAUCES

Hard sauces make dessert time a happier occasion. They are usually made with butter and powdered sugar, along with other ingredients, and then refrigerated until used. Usually they are served cold over hot dishes such as puddings and custards.

Hard sauces can also be melted in a chafing dish and used as a poaching sauce for many kinds of fruits. Bananas, peaches and pears lend themselves particularly well to this method of dessert-making.

On the next two pages you will find a trio of hard sauce recipes which will please the most difficult to please.

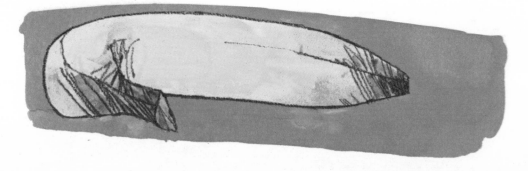

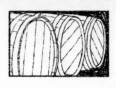

BRANDY HARD SAUCE

1/2 cup sweet butter
1-1/2 cups powdered sugar
3 tablespoons brandy

Cream the butter until soft, using your electric beater. Then, with the beater at low speed, slowly beat in the powdered sugar, then add the brandy. Freshly ground nutmeg on top is a nice final touch. Chill before serving.

SPICY HARD SAUCE

Follow the directions in the recipe on the facing page, substituting brown sugar for powdered, and adding 3 tablespoons of extra strong black coffee.

1/2 cup sweet butter
1-1/2 cups powdered sugar
3 tablespoons brandy
1/8 teaspoon cinnamon, ground

Make this sauce the same way as described on the facing page, adding the cinnamon last.

Cocktails, Flips & Punches

Brandy has been consumed as a beverage, both by itself and mixed with other liquids and flavors, for hundreds of years. It was a favorite drink in American colonial times when George Washington, Thomas Jefferson and John Adams often forsook their glass of Madeira for a small snifter of well-made brandy.

In this second half of the 20th Century, consumption of brandy as a beverage, and as an ingredient in ever-increasing numbers of recipes and combinations, is rising at a rate greater than any other type of liquor.

On the pages which follow, you will find a generous sampling of recipes for brandy in old combinations and new.

Unless otherwise specified, as in the case of the punches, all recipes are for a single drink.

AMERICAN COCKTAIL

Fill a highball glass half full of crushed ice. Add 1 oz. of brandy, 1 oz. of Fernet-Branca (an Italian bitters) and fill with soda.

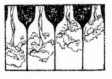

BRANDY BOMB

Fill a shaker 1/4 full of crushed ice. Add 1/2 teaspoon sugar, 2 dashes of Angostura bitters, 2 dashes of Curacao and 1-1/2 oz of brandy. Stir and strain into a cocktail glass.

144

SATAN COCKTAIL

Fill a shaker 1/4 full of crushed ice. Add 1 oz. of green creme de menthe, 1 oz. of brandy, 2 oz. of Curacao and a pinch of cayenne pepper. Stir vigorously and strain into a cocktail glass.

METRO COCKTAIL

Fill shaker 1/4 full of crushed ice. Add 2 dashes of orange bitters, a tablespoon of simple syrup, 1 oz. of brandy, and 3/4 oz of dry vermouth. Stir and strain into a cocktail glass.

SAUTERNE SURPRISE

Into a highball glass 1/2 filled with crushed ice, pour 1/2 oz. of raspberry syrup, 3 dashes of Curacao, and 1 oz. of brandy. Now add 1 small piece of peeled and chilled fruit, in season, and fill up the glass with chilled sauterne.

BRANDY FIZZ

Fill a small shaker 1/4 full of crushed ice and add 1 tablespoon powdered sugar, 1 tablespoon egg white, the juice of half a lemon, and 1 oz. of brandy. Shake, strain into a highball glass, then add club soda to fill the glass.

BRANDY GROG

Fill a shaker 1/2 full of crushed ice, add 1 teaspoon powdered sugar, 1 fresh egg, well beaten, and 1-1/2 oz. of brandy. Shake and strain into a 4 oz. glass and top with ground nutmeg.

BRANDY FLIP

Into a grog glass, put 1/2 tablespoon granulated sugar, 1-1/4 oz. of brandy and fill with boiling water. Top with a single lemon slice.

COLD BRANDY PUNCH

To a shaker 3/4 filled with crushed ice, add 1 teaspoon orange juice, 1 tablespoon powdered sugar, 1 tablespoon cold water, 1 oz. of light rum and 1-1/4 oz. of brandy. Shake and strain into a highball glass.

HOT BRANDY PUNCH

Into a heated grog glass or short highball glass, put 1 teaspoon of lemon juice, 1 tablespoon powdered sugar, 2 dashes of Curacao, and 1 oz. of brandy. Fill with boiling water, stir well and top with nutmeg.

HOT MILK PUNCH

Into a highball glass put 1 tablespoon of powdered sugar, 1 oz. of brandy and 1 oz. of light rum. Fill with hot, but not boiling milk, stir and top with nutmeg.

COLD MILK PUNCH

Same as above except use cold milk and 1/2 tablespoon of granulated sugar instead of the full tablespoon of powdered sugar.

149

PUNCHES

Huge punch bowls filled with a variety of imaginative drinks are part of our heritage from our European forefathers, and make almost any occasion festive.

Punch is believed to have originated among English sailors. There is a story of one English sea captain who prepared a monster punch made of 80 casks of brandy, nine casks of water, 25,000 large limes, 80 pints of lemon juice, 1300 pounds of sugar, five pounds of nutmeg and one large cask of Malaga wine. To serve the 6000 guests from such a vast marble basin, small boys used a rowboat floating on that vast alcoholic sea, but the fumes overcame them and they had to be replaced every fifteen minutes.

TASTE AS YOU GO

Whenever you make a punch for the first time a precise recipe is helpful, if not essential, and so I share with you the specifics on the following pages. However, you are the best judge of the exact taste which will please you and your guests, so I recommend that you "taste as you go" when mixing any punch. Your objective is to achieve your own master blend each time you make a batch. Generally, you'll have greater success when you make each new batch separately, rather than to add a little of this or that because the bowl is half empty. Happy mixing! And tasting!

CHAMPAGNE PUNCH A LA ANTOINE'S

1 bottle of champagne
1 bottle of sauterne
1/4 lb. of powdered sugar
1 pint of sparkling water
1 cup brandy
2 oz. of Maraschino
2 oz. of Cointreau
1 block of ice
thin slices of orange peel and pineapple

Mix well in a punch bowl; add a block of ice, thin slices of peeled orange and fresh pineapple. Makes 25 to 30 servings.

CHAMPAGNE PUNCH

Here is another punch which will easily accommodate 50 people.

6 bottles of chilled champagne
2 bottles of chilled sauterne
6 lemons, peeled and sliced
6 oranges, peeled and sliced
6 fresh mint leaves
1 cup granulated sugar

35 sticks of fresh pineapple,
   1 inch x 3 inches
large block of ice
2 cups of brandy
2 quarts fresh strawberries

Into a large punch bowl pour 3 bottles of the champagne and all of the sauterne. Add lemons, oranges, mint leaves, sugar, and the pineapple. Stir well. Put in the ice, brandy, stawberries, mix well, then add the 3 remaining bottles of champagne.

BRANDY COFFEE PUNCH

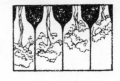

Many times the combination of two favorite drinks produces a special drink that gets rave notices. Certainly coffee and brandy, generally served separately, have historically been cousins. In this recipe, we have married them.

2 quarts of hot coffee
peel of 1 orange
peel of 1 lemon
1/2 cup sugar

1 pint of brandy
1/2 pint whipping cream
2 tablespoons confectioner's sugar

Combine coffee, orange and lemon peel, and sugar. Cool for several hours. When it is time to serve your guests, remove orange and lemon peel and pour coffee into a punch bowl. Stir in brandy. Whip cream with confectioner's sugar. Serve coffee in punch cups and top with big spoonful of whipped cream. Makes 16 servings.

SATAN'S PUNCH

The use of dry ice makes this already gala punch even more so.

12 bottles of champagne
1 fifth of brandy
12 limes, peeled and sliced thin
12 strawberries, whole
12 bottles of sauterne
1 slab of dry ice — 4 x 6 inches

This recipe makes about 150 punch-cup servings. You may want to make it in two batches and if you do, simply halve the ingredients each time. Put everything into the punch bowl in the order listed, mix a little, then add the dry ice. The ice produces a beautiful bubbling effect and is quite harmless. It is dramatic showmanship.

CAFE GRECO'S PUNCH ALL LIVORNESE

In Rome's Cafe Greco on the Via Condotti, there is a warm drink named Punch all Livornese that is served year around to thirsty friends. While it is called a punch by the owners, each drink is individually made. So instead of composing a punch bowl recipe for you, here is the recipe just as it is served at Cafe Greco.

One 4 oz. wine glass
sugar to taste
1 small lemon peel
1/2 cup hot coffee
1 tablespoon brandy

Preheat the wine glass by pouring boiling water into it. Within a few seconds the glass will be hot. Pour out water. Add sugar, lemon peel, coffee and brandy. Stir and serve.

INNOCENT PUNCH

6 lumps of sugar
a dash of Angostura bitters
1-1/2 cups brandy
4 bottles of chilled champagne
6 slices each, of lemon, orange and lime
1 block of ice

Put the sugar cubes in the bottom of the punch bowl, add the bitters and the brandy. When your guests arrive, pour the champagne into the bowl, add a block of ice and float the fruit on top. Serves 20 people.

WEDDING PUNCH

No collection of recipes for punch would be complete without one strictly for a wedding. I consider this one appropriately festive and it is my favorite.

4 limes, thinly sliced
1/2 cup sugar
grated rind of 2 lemons
1 cup orange juice
1/2 cup lemon juice
2 fifths brandy
2 cups of Cointreau
5 bottles of dry champagne
1 block of ice

In your punch bowl, mix everything together except the Cointreau and the champagne. Let this mixture stand for at least an hour in your refrigerator. If you cannot get the bowl into the refrigerator, you can pour the mixture into several pitchers and then refrigerate. When guests arrive bring out the bowl (or refill it from the pitchers), add a block of ice, the Cointreau, and the champagne. Serve in about 10 minutes. This will serve about 35 guests through a normal reception. You may want to have several bowls about, each with the full recipe, depending upon the number of guests.

EGGNOGS

While champagne is used in punches for all seasons, the combination of eggs, brandy and sugar in eggnogs is usually with us at year's end. In most of America and many parts of western Europe eggnogs are happily and warmly consumed at Christmas time and New Year's.

On the next three pages are recipes for one simple eggnog to be made individually and for one fancy eggnog to be made for 30.

BRANDY EGGNOG

2 egg yolks
2 tablespoons powdered sugar
2 oz. of brandy
milk

Into a warmed glass or punch cup, put the egg yolks, sugar and the brandy. Fill with hot milk, stir, and sprinkle with grated nutmeg, preferably fresh.

CALIFORNIA EGGNOG

10 eggs, separated
3/4 cup granulated sugar
4 cups of whole milk, scalded
a giant pinch of salt
1 cup whipped cream
3/4 cup brandy
grated nutmeg to taste

In the top of a double boiler, beat the 10 egg yolks. Blend in 1/2 cup of sugar and stir in the scalded milk. Cook over hot water until the mixture is thick. Now add salt to 10 egg whites and beat until they peak and are stiff. Mix the remaining 1/4 cup of sugar into the egg whites and fold the whites into the egg yolk mixture. When mixed, fold in the whipped cream, add the brandy and chill for three hours. When you are ready to serve, pour the eggnog into a chilled punch bowl. Top with freshly grated nutmeg. This recipe will make 20 punch-cup servings.

OTHER BRANDY DRINKS

Because brandy is a product of the grape, it is almost infinitely mixable in cocktails. I encourage you to experiment by substituting brandy in any drink in which you presently use whiskey.

If you like whiskey and water—you will probably like brandy and water. If you enjoy whiskey Manhattans—try a brandy Manhattan. Even if you prefer combining your whiskey with 7-up or ginger ale, you may very well discover that brandy is most enjoyable with the same mixers.

A small glass—or an elegant snifter—of brandy after dinner or later in the evening is a tradition in many American and European homes.

Menus

A recipe book such as this is invaluable to any person responsible for preparing meals and entertaining in the home. But the true expert culinary performer is the one who coordinates a complete meal and the final result is a well-balanced, nutritious menu.

On the pages immediately following are seven varied menus which include a selection of recipes in this book. Obviously, not all dishes are improved by the addition of brandy, so you will find courses and complements in these menus for which you will not find the recipe here. These are marked with an asterisk (*).

I have served these particular menus many times to the pleasure of my family and my friends; I've also varied them with equal pleasure and I urge you to try them as written and with your own variations.

A VINTNER'S LUNCH

Champagne
Chicken Breasts with Brandy (page 80)
(Vegetables of your Choice)
Cafe Brulot (page 131)
Suggested Wine: Pinot Chardonnay

A SPRING DINNER FOR SIX

Brandied Olives (page 8)
Nail Soup (page 23)
*Roast Beef
*Cauliflower with Bacon   *Peas with Butter Sauce
Salad with Stilton Cheese Dressing (page 106)
Brandy Bings (page 122)
Coffee
Suggested Wine: Pinot Noir

A SIMPLE CALIFORNIA REPAST

Tartare Steak Genghis Khan (page 12)
Cioppino San Francisco Style (page 20)
French Bread
Fire Peaches (page 125)
Coffee
Suggested Wine: Chenin Blanc

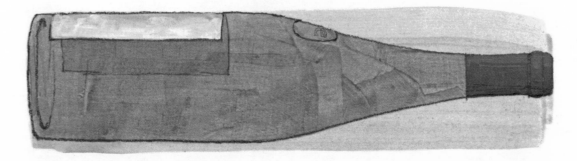

AN AUTUMN PICNIC

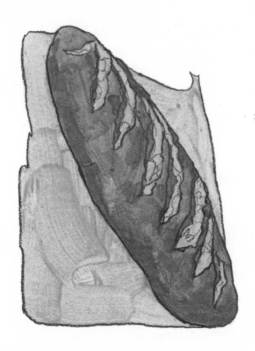

Champagne
Country Paté (page 48)
French Bread
*Carrot Sticks   *Celery Sticks
*Potato Salad
Fresh Fruit
Cheese
Suggested Wine: Barbera

AN INFORMAL DINNER

Metro Cocktail (page 145)
Poor Man's Minestrone (page 17)
Chicken O'Farrel (page 78)
Vegetables of Your Choice
Salad with Brandy Mayonnaise (page 105)
Chocolate Cream Pots (page 118)
Coffee
Suggested Wine: Johannisberg Reisling

DINNER FOR FOUR

Mozzarella in Carozza (page 13)
Brandy Fizz (page 146)
Filet of Sole-Brandy & Bitters (page 60)
*Boiled New Potatoes
Vegetables of your Choice
Salad with Roquefort Dressing (page 106)
Iced Brandy Grapes (page 124)
Suggested Wine: Grey Reisling

INFORMAL SUNDAY DINNER

Satan Cocktails (page 145)
Brandy Consomme (page 18)
Pepper Steak (page 28)
*Carrots Glace
Green Salad with Romano Dressing (page 106)
Bananas Flambe Hebert (page 116)
Coffee
Suggested Wine: Cabernet Sauvignon

A SUMMER LUNCH

Mushrooms Montebello (page 10)
Consomme de Foie Gras (page 16)
Spit-Roasted Chicken
Basted with Butter, Brandy & Anise (page 76)
Coffee
Suggested Wine: Rose

What & Where is Brandy ?

The word "brandy" evolved from "brandewine," which was borrowed from the Dutch "brandewijn." In Dutch, "branden" means to burn, or to distill, and "wijn" is the word for wine.

Historians record that distillation of wine into brandy occurred much earlier in the East than in Western civilization. The Italians had brandy in the 13th Century and the Moors introduced brandy-making in Spain during their occupation. By mid 17th Century, brandy was available over most of Europe.

Brandy making in the United States probably began with the Mission Fathers who first brought grapevines to California. Captain John Sutter, at whose mill the discovery of gold started the Gold Rush, was operating a fully equipped brandy still at his fort in 1843.

While there are brandies made from other fruits such as cherries, peaches, and a number of berries, all of which are properly called "Fruit Brandy," the liquor distilled from wine made from grapes is called, simply, "brandy" and it is this liquor alone that this book features in the recipes.

The best brandies are distilled from the wine of grapes with high sugar content and no distinct varietal flavor. As the brandy comes out of the still, it is a clear liquid and is stored and aged in oak casks from which it takes on its amber or brown color. All effective aging takes place in the cask--once bottled, brandy no longer improves with age. Variations in brandies are the result of different grapes, different oaks in the aging cask, length of aging, and blending formulae.

Brandy had been made in California in modest amounts since the arrival of the first white man, but with the repeal of Prohibition in 1933, its popularity increased with each passing year.

Today there are thousands of acres planted in grapes specifically for brandy making, stretching from Lodi, east of San Francisco, 200 miles south through Fresno and Bakersfield, to the end of the San Joaquin Valley. In this warm and fertile valley, the soil, climate, and the skills of the vintners and distillers combine to make a superbly unique American liquor.

There are over 300 different brands of California brandy accounting for 98% of all United States production. Some are heavy and fruity . . . others are light and dry . . . all are wonderful for cooking and drinking.

Index

Other Nitty Gritty Cookbooks

Italian
Cheese
Miller's German
Quiche & Souffle
To My Daughter, With Love
Natural Foods
Four Seasons Party
Jewish Gourmet
Working Couples
Mexican
Paris . . . and then some
Sunday Breakfast
Fisherman's Wharf
Charcoal
Ice Cream
Hamburger
Gourmet Blender
Christmas
Cast Iron
Japanese
Soul Food
Fondue

If you have enjoyed this Brandy Cookbook, you may enjoy other titles on our Nitty Gritty list.

Use the order form below -- take it (or mail with $3.95 for each book) to your local book or gift store.

Name_____

Address_____

City_____   State_____   Zip_____

Enclosed $ _____

Nitty Gritty Productions
P.O.Box 5457,Concord, CA.94524